THE KID'S GUIDE TO NEW YORK CITY

3rd
edition

Eileen Ogintz

Globe Pequot

Guilford, Connecticut

Special thanks to my daughter Melanie Yemma and Nora Brown, who was raised in Brooklyn. for their research help. Thanks also to the NYC kids at the American Museum of Natural History's Lang Science Program for their insights and to CityPASS for the passes that facilitated research.

All the information in this guidebook is subject to change. We recommend that you call ahead to obtain current information before traveling.

Globe Pequot

An imprint of Rowman & Littlefield
Distributed by NATIONAL BOOK NETWORK

Copyright © 2016 by Eileen Ogintz
Illustrations licensed by Shutterstock.com

British Library Cataloguing in Publication Information Available

Library of Congress Cataloging-in-Publication Data Available

ISBN 978-1-4930-2387-5 (paperback)
ISBN 978-1-4930-2388-2 (e-book)

 The paper used in this publication meets the minimum requirements of American National Standard for Information Sciences—Permanence of Paper for Printed Library Materials, ANSI/NISO Z39.48-1992.

Contents

1

Say Hello to the Big Apple!

Ready to take a big bite out of the Big Apple?

There is so much to do here that you are guaranteed to have fun—sports, art, science, music, theater, and more! You can also take your pick of any food. And it will be great.

Check out all the big buildings. This is one place you won't get bored. In fact, there's so much to do it's impossible to do it all no matter how long you stay.

That's why New York is always tops on kids' lists of places they want to visit. Listen to all the different languages that people are speaking. The experts say 160 different ones, everything from Arabic to Spanish to Chinese, Russian, and Hebrew. But New York is also home to

> ## A NYC KID SAYS:
> "I've got friends who are Chinese, Korean, Puerto Rican, Mexican, African American, Jewish, Indian . . . and a lot of others, too."
> —Regan, 11, NYC

What's Cool? You can always find something to eat—right on the street. New York kids love soft pretzels from the street vendors. You'll also see vendors and trucks selling kabobs, ice cream, cupcakes, and Italian ice. Visit nyctruckfood.com and take your pick . . .

How Did New York Get Its Name?

The Algonquin Indians and other tribes were the first New Yorkers, here when Henry Hudson showed up in 1609. He was actually looking for a passageway to the Orient when he stumbled into New York Harbor. Fifteen years later, the Dutch had settled here and named the area New Amsterdam. But by 1674, the English were in charge, and they renamed the busy settlement New York after James, Duke of York.

A NYC KID SAYS:
"One of my favorite NYC souvenirs is the subway shirt. You can buy them for a friend with the letter of their name!"
—Brian, 12, NYC

millions of parents and kids. Many of them have come from around the world to live here. No matter what they wear or what language they speak, they're all still New Yorkers.

What's Cool? You might be able to be on TV if you get up really early and hold up a funny sign outside a broadcasting studio. Head to NBC's Studios at Rockefeller Center (just off Fifth Avenue between 49th and 50th Streets) to join the crowd at *The Today Show*. You can join the crowd at *Good Morning America* in Times Square. There are other shows filmed in NYC too. The website nytix.com can tell you how to get tickets.

Ask a New York kid on his way to school or in a museum to point you to the nearest playground or place to get a bagel.

A VISITING KID SAYS:
"I was really surprised how easy it is to get around on subways and buses!"
—Jake, 9, Aspen, CO

So where do you want to go first? *The Kid's Guide to New York City* helps you have the most fun! We've asked kids to help, too. You'll see their ideas in every chapter.

GOT A MAP?

Manhattan is split into the East Side and the West Side by Fifth Avenue. You'll hear people talk about the Upper East Side and Upper West Side as if they were different countries! A lot of kids also live in Brooklyn, the Bronx, Staten Island, and Queens. It's easier to understand New York if you think of it as a lot of little neighborhoods. You'll also hear some other funny names of neighborhoods, and if you know what they mean, you're on your way to becoming a New Yorker!

Pick places within one neighborhood to explore at one time. Your feet won't get nearly so tired!

SUBWAYS & BUSES

Got comfy shoes? The best way to get around NYC is on foot—or on public transportation. Subways are the quickest—the first subway car is always the most fun—but you can see where you're going on the bus. Make sure you've

{ **What's Cool?** Look at all the amazing architecture in New York! Draw a picture of your
favorite building.

TELL THE ADULTS:

- **MTA Bus Time** (bustime.mta.info) shows you
the location of the next bus. **Embark NYC**
(letsembark.com) lets you know when the train
is coming.

got a yellow **MetroCard** to pay for your ride. Check out the big subway maps that are posted in every train station. It's fun to follow your route with a pocket map found at any train station—or check outmta.info and click on "Trip Planner." Check out the tile walls along some of the platforms—they're often the work of local artists.

DID YOU KNOW?

To hail a taxi, tell your parents to stand next to the curb and wave really hard. Don't forget to buckle your seatbelt when you get inside. A lot of families also use UBER (uber.com) to catch a ride.

The Dutch bought Manhattan Island from the Indians in 1626 for about $24 worth of tools and necklaces. See what you can buy in NYC today for $24.

TELL THE ADULTS:

- Leave lots of time to explore the city's neighborhoods as well as museums! That's where you'll discover the real New York—from coffee shops and delis to playgrounds and firehouses. Stop by a firehouse. New York firefighters will be glad to show you around—if they're not off fighting a fire!

- Make sure each member of the family picks out where you're going and what you're doing each day.

- NYMETROPARENTS (metroparents.com) is a good resource as is TimeOut (timeout.com/new-york-kids) to find out special happenings at the time you are in the city.

A VISITING KID SAYS:
"My favorite thing to do in NYC is travel around the city and window-shop."
—Brendan, 13, ME

2

New York City's
Neighborhoods

Get your sneakers on!

The best way to see the way kids live in New York is to walk around the city's neighborhoods. And you'll want to wear your comfiest shoes.

Ask kids you see to point you to their favorite playground or pizza place in the neighborhood. They'll know— just like you would at home.

Even if you get to stroll through just one or two city neighborhoods, you'll realize New York is a lot more than skyscrapers, restaurants, and big stores.

- Alphabet City is named for avenues A, B, C, and D.

- Chelsea was named after a fancy neighborhood in London.

- Chinatown has become the biggest Asian community in North America.

- Flatiron District is named after the building on Broadway and 23rd Street whose top looks like an old-fashioned iron.

- **Greenwich Village** started out as a 17th-century suburb, a green village. Today it's full of people, cafes, clubs, shops, and New York University.

- **Ground Zero** is the area of Lower Manhattan destroyed in 2001. The Freedom Tower was built here and opened to the public in 2015 and the National September 11 Memorial was opened to the public on September 12, 2011. There are special activity stations for kids at the 9/11 Memorial Museum (180 Greenwich St.; 212-312-8800; 911memorial.org.

- **Harlem** is north of 110th Street and has long been a hub of New York's African-American community.

- **Little Italy** is home to many Italian Americans and the site of some great Italian restaurants.

- **Lower East Side** was once the center of Jewish life in New York, now is known for its stores, hip restaurants, and shopping deals. This is one part of New York where you can still bargain!

- **Midtown** is just what it sounds like—the middle of town where there are lots of skyscrapers, restaurants, businesses, and stores.

- **Nolita** means "North of Little Italy" and that's where this trendy neighborhood is located.

- **SoHo** means South of Houston Street. (New Yorkers pronounce it "HOW-ston.") It has lots of art galleries and stores. You might want to stop in at the **New York City Fire Museum** (278 Spring St.; 212-691-1303; nycfiremuseum.org) while you're in the neighborhood

DID YOU KNOW?

2.5 million people live on Brooklyn—nearly a million more than live on Manhattan Island.

to see how New York firemen have always done their jobs and the old hand-pulled and horse-drawn engines they used in the old days.

> ## A NYC KID SAYS:
> "Every kid who visits NYC should not miss Brooklyn Bridge Park—it's one of the coolest parks I've ever been to. It's super cool to see and play volleyball at and rollerblade for free!"
> —Josh, 10, Brooklyn

DID YOU KNOW?

You can walk or bike from Manhattan to Brooklyn across the **Brooklyn Bridge**. It's about a mile. The bridge took 16 years to build in the late 1800s.

- **Times Square** at 42nd Street and Broadway is the heart of the theater district—and where you'll find the most souvenir shops.

- **TriBeCa,** on the Lower West Side, is short for "Triangle Below Canal (Street)."

- **Upper East Side** (North of 59th Street and east of Central Park) has some of New York's fanciest apartment buildings as well as a lot of shopping at stores such as Bloomingdale's.

- **Upper West Side** (North of 59th Street and everything west of Central Park) is the area that includes the American Museum of Natural History, a kids' favorite.

Brooklyn and Beyond

Young hipsters-to-be will want to head to Williamsburg, in Brooklyn. But there's plenty else for families here, including:

- **Coney Island**, where New Yorkers have been coming for more than a century for fun, including the wooden Cyclone rollercoaster, the beach boardwalk, and the New York Aquarium. It's also where the Brooklyn Cyclones play minor league baseball (Surf Avenue & Stillwell Avenue, Brooklyn, NY 11224; coneyislandfunguide.com).

- **The Brooklyn Children's Museum**, with daily special programs as well as plenty of free fun exhibits (145 Brooklyn Ave., Brooklyn NY 11213; 718-735-4400; brooklynkids.org/visit).

- **The Brooklyn Botanical Garden**, with its discovery garden designed for young naturalists with hands-on experiences in a meadow, marsh, vegetable garden, and more. In the summer there are special Kids' Discovery Stations (several entrances, including 455 Flatbush Ave., Brooklyn NY 11225).

- **The Barclays Center** is the multipurpose arena where the NBA's Brooklyn Nets and the New York Islanders NHL team play (620 Atlantic Ave., Brooklyn, NY 11217; barclayscenter.com).

- **Prospect Park**, in the heart of Brooklyn with outdoor summer concerts, birdwatching, the Prospect Park Zoo, boating, biking, greenmarket, playgrounds, the Audubon Center, carousel, and the innovative play area—the Zucker Natural Exploration Area (95 Prospect Park West, Brooklyn, NY 11215; 718-965-8951).

- **The Brooklyn Museum**, New York's second largest, with a collection of 1.5 million works from ancient Egyptian masterpieces to contemporary art, and special "Arty" Facts programs on Sundays for young kids 4-7 (200 Eastern Pkwy., Brooklyn, NY 11238; 718-638-5000).

A lot of kids who visit New York also like to head downtown, especially to eat, shop, and people-watch. Many families live downtown, too.

Greenwich Village—a lot of people just call it "The Village"—has lots of little stores, cafes, and parks, as well as New York University. You'll see a lot of students in Washington Square Park and parents with kids who live in the neighborhood.

If you love sports, head toward the Hudson River, and in between 17th and 23rd Streets you'll find the **Chelsea Piers Sports and Entertainment Complex**

DID YOU KNOW?

The Bronx is the only one of New York's five boroughs connected to the mainland. To get to Manhattan, Queens, Staten Island, or Brooklyn you have to take a tunnel or a bridge.

Most NYC neighborhoods are only about 10 square blocks. They've got ice cream shops, pizza parlors, parks, schools, and lots of families and pets.

For some kids, their apartment building is like your block at home. They play with kids in their building and make friends with the doorman whose job it is to keep track of who goes in and out. They also go trick-or-treating in their building on Halloween!

(chelseapiers.com). The complex is on four different historic piers over the river, and you can take your pick from 17 different sports to play, from rock climbing to ice-skating to sailing to soccer and more!

Very close to the piers is **The High Line** (thehighline.org), a park built on top of old New York City freight train tracks. The park runs from Gansevoort Street in the Meatpacking District to West 34th Street, between 10th and 12th Avenues. You'll find restaurants, places to get ice cream, and all kinds of special activities.

Head south of the Village for more shopping and eating in SoHo, Little Italy, Chinatown, and the Lower East Side, once the biggest Jewish community in the world that today has lots of hip shops and restaurants.

Many kids move to New York every year from other countries with their families—from Asia, Africa, India, the Caribbean Islands, and Central America, among other places. They're part of what makes New York so great.

{ What's Cool? The special activities for kids on the High Line and the chance to stargaze through high-powered telescopes every Tuesday evening April – October. Visit thehighline.org for more details.

The Bronx Zoo

Ready to get up close and personal with the animals?

At the Bronx Zoo (2300 Southern Blvd., Bronx, NY 10460; 718-220-5100; bronxzoo.com). Take your pick.

You can head to the African rain forest and visit more than 20 gorillas in the Congo Gorilla Forest. Maybe you'd rather meet Siberian tigers at Tiger Mountain. In the summer, you can wander amid 1,000 different kinds of butterflies and moths. Check out a black leopard in JungleWorld, an endangered snow leopard in the Himalayan habitat, or see all the little rodents in the Mouse House. Take the Bengali Express Monorail through Wild Asia, past tigers, elephants, rhinos, antelopes, and more.

There's a lot of ground to cover, and you won't want to miss anything. There is a Zoo Shuttle you can take from one

A VISITING KID SAYS:
"Don't worry about transportation. It's really easy to get around. I was surprised!"
—Jake, 9, Aspen, CO

part of the zoo to another and a Skyfari gondola that gets you from Asia to the Children's Zoo in no time.

At the Children's Zoo, open April through October, kids can climb into child-size heron nests, walk through a prairie dog tunnel, or climb a 20-foot spider web made of rope. In the forest, climb up the platform 14 feet high to get face-to-face with a porcupine or look through a telescope. Remember to stop and feed the goats.

For more than 100 years, this zoo has been welcoming kids and parents. It's also a center for conservation.

Besides seeing the animals, here's your chance to learn about how you can help.

What's your favorite animal?

{ **What's Cool?** There are hundreds of baby animals born every year at the Bronx Zoo.

TELL THE ADULTS:

- FREE IS GOOD! Many city museums have free admission nights and free family guides. Check their websites before visiting.

- Big Apple Greeter (212-669-8159; bigapplegreeter. org) offers FREE tours to visiting families and gives you all their top picks in their favorite neighborhoods. You need to make an appointment several weeks in advance.

- NYC Parks (nycgovparks.org), including the Brooklyn Bridge Park (brooklynbridgepark) on the waterfront, has become a mecca for families since it opened, complete with bike trails, playgrounds, sand volleyball courts, and even a beach.

- For budding fashionistas, the Fashion Institute of Technology Museum features rotating exhibits by students and a gallery of fashion, dating back to the 18th century. (fitnyc.edu/museum.asp; Seventh Avenue and 27th Street; 212-217-4558).

- The National Museum of the American Indian—New York, the George Gustav Heye Center, has exhibits, daily hands-on activities, and, performing arts center. (Alexander Hamilton U.S. Custom House, One Bowling

Green, New York, NY 10004; 212-514-3700; nmai.si.edu/explore/forfamilies).

- The New York Public Library (42nd Street and Fifth Avenue), where there is a Children's Center with ongoing programs for families, including storytelling and guest appearances by authors.

- The Schomburg Center for Research in Black Culture, part of the city's library center, has the largest collection of everything from documents to art to recordings related to the African-American experience (515 Malcolm X Blvd, New York, NY 10037; 917-275-6975; nypl.org/locations/schomburg).

- KAYAK for free in the summer from the Downtown Boathouse at several locations including Pier 96 (56th Street in Hudson River Park) and 72nd Street, north of Pier I café in Riverside Park. (downtown boathouse.org/free-kayaking/).

- The Federal Reserve Bank of New York, where you can see the gold vault, the world's largest accumulation of gold—as long as you reserve a guided tour in advance (33 Liberty St., New York, NY 10045; 212-720-6130, newyorkfed.org/aboutthefed/visiting.html).

Stories Everywhere!

There are NYC libraries (nypl.org) all over the city, and in them you'll find many stories that take place in New York. Do you have a favorite? Here are some that NYC librarians think you'd like:

The Adventures of Taxi Dog by Debra and Sal Barracca

Eloise by Kay Thompson, the story of a six-year-old who grows up in the Plaza Hotel

Lyle, Lyle Crocodile by Bernard Waber is about a NYC family who find a crocodile named Lyle in their bathtub!

The Cricket in Times Square by George Selden follows the adventures of a cricket who ends up in Times Square.

Stuart Little by E.B. White is the story of a NYC family's little mouse and takes place all around Central Park.

Harriet the Spy by Louise Fitzhugh follows the adventures of a sixth-grader who lives in Manhattan.

From the Mixed-up Files of Mrs. Basil E. Frankweiler by E.L. Konigsburg tells the story of two Connecticut kids who camp out in the Metropolitan Museum and solve a mystery.

What's your favorite book set in New York?

Movies Everywhere!

Lots of movies and TV shows are set in NYC and many are filmed here. Just a few of them include:

Spider-Man
Superman
Batman
Home Alone 2
Miracle on 34th Street
Ghostbusters
Stepmom
Stuart Little
Sesame Street

How many other New York–based movies can you name?

_____

_____

_____

_____

_____

_____

_____

_____

_____

_____

Harlem

More than a third of the length of Manhattan is north of 110th Street, and that includes Harlem. First settled in the 1600s by Dutch tobacco farmers, Harlem in the 1920s was the most famous black community in the country, maybe in the world. Many African Americans still live there, and it's fast becoming a hot neighborhood again with new stores, restaurants, and attractions. Think you want to be a star? The **Apollo Theater** at 253 125th St. in Harlem has started to hold "amateur nights" to find new stars (for more information, visit apollotheater.org). If you're a dancer, you might want to see a performance at the **Dance Theatre of Harlem** (466 West 152nd St.; 212-690-2800; dancetheatreofharlem.org).

DID YOU KNOW?

The name **Manhattan** comes from a Native American word that means "the place of hills."

NYC's nickname, **The Big Apple**, came from a tourism campaign in 1971, and it has stuck ever since.

A NYC KID SAYS:
"Go to the parks. They are always relaxing!"
—Sam, 13, NYC

WORD SEARCH

Find some of the neighborhoods and boroughs of NYC
(Words are horizontal, vertical, and diagonal.)

Brooklyn
Chinatown
Greenwich
 Village
Ground Zero
Harlem

Little Italy
Lower East Side
Manhattan
Midtown
Queens
SoHo

Staten Island
The Bronx
Times Square
TriBeCa

```
S  T  S  M  U  X  O  M  D  S  D  X  Y  R  J  E  N
T  I  O  A  A  H  E  M  S  N  T  L  W  K  G  T  B
A  M  T  N  J  L  S  G  P  Y  A  B  Z  A  D  H  R
T  E  G  H  R  V  O  W  F  T  V  L  L  W  J  E  O
E  S  K  A  Q  T  H  P  I  W  R  L  S  N  Z  B  O
N  S  H  T  Z  M  O  E  E  J  I  B  D  I  O  R  K
I  Q  I  T  J  H  L  S  F  V  X  Y  N  S  N  O  L
S  U  E  A  Z  T  L  R  H  H  R  L  X  R  T  N  Y
L  A  V  N  T  E  K  C  Z  V  T  G  H  L  R  X  N
A  R  E  I  W  K  I  G  R  O  U  N  D  Z  E  R  O
N  E  L  E  X  W  Z  E  A  F  O  H  R  N  N  X  J
D  M  R  E  N  E  D  I  S  M  I  D  T  O  W  N  Q
H  I  H  E  M  C  H  I  N  A  T  O  W  N  E  Q  U
C  T  E  V  L  O  W  E  R  E  A  S  T  S  I  D  E
G  R  N  T  R  C  L  W  T  X  N  V  U  H  Q  W  E
G  K  T  D  T  R  I  B  E  C  A  Q  I  M  X  O  N
U  N  S  P  U  O  D  W  K  B  R  N  S  F  B  R  S
```

See page 138 for the answer key.

3

Mummies, Knights, & All Kinds of Art

Name the place in New York

where you can time travel from ancient Egypt to Japan, from Europe hundreds of years ago to the US today.

Stumped? The answer is **The Metropolitan Museum of Art** (Fifth Avenue and 82nd Street; 212-535-7710; metmuseum.org). It's so big that from end to end, the museum stretches four New York City blocks—a quarter of a mile! There are more than 90 bathrooms!

The Met, as New Yorkers call it, has been around for more than 130 years. When you walk in the enormous front doors, you're entering one of the biggest and best art museums in the world. And even if you think you hate museums, this one can be fun as long as you know where to go. Of course, you can't possibly see everything in one visit!

DID YOU KNOW?

The **Brooklyn Children's Museum** (145 Brooklyn Ave., Brooklyn, NY; 718-735-4400; brooklynkids.org) was the first museum created just for kids. That was in 1899, and since then, hundreds of children's museums have opened around the world. There is also a **Children's Museum of Manhattan** (212 W. 83rd St.; 212-721-1223; cmom.org).

The Met has special family guides to the museum that you can download from its website, metmuseum.org, or you can pick them up at the information desk when you arrive.

And when you get tired, you can run and play all you want in Central Park just outside.

A lot of kids head for the ancient Egyptian Temple of Dendur first. In fact, it's one of the most popular exhibits in the entire museum. The temple, built in 15 BC, was taken apart in Egypt and transported by ship to New York. Engineers had to make detailed drawings so they would know how to put it back together to match how it appeared on the banks of the Nile River. If it had not been moved, it would have been covered by waters rising behind a new dam that was being built. The government of Egypt was very happy the temple could be brought to New York and gave it to our government as a present. The Met built an entire area to house the temple.

Kids also like to see the mummies that are in galleries in the main building near the Temple of Dendur. Thirteen of the mummies contain bodies, twelve of them adults and one child. We know that because museum experts did scans—similar to X-rays—of the mummies.

A VISITING KID SAYS:
"My favorite thing was the temple from Egypt they took apart and brought here to the Met. I don't know how they did it!"
—James, 11, Aspen, CO

Have you ever imagined being a Knight in Shining Armor, fighting battles with a big sword? You might not want to after you stop to see the Met's collection of Arms and Armor. Those suits were heavy! So were the weapons!

Kids especially like the Costume Institute. You can see the kind of clothes people wore in different countries and a long time ago.

Of course, you're not going to leave without seeing some paintings and sculptures. Take your pick—impressionist art from France, sculptures from the US, African masks, or Chinese porcelain. What part of the world do you want to visit today?

TELL THE ADULTS

Visiting an art museum can be a real adventure! Many NYC museums like the Metropolitan offer special family workshops for kids of different ages, exhibit guides, and apps for touring particular exhibits. There are also special programs for kids with special challenges. For example, the Met offers Drop-In drawing the 1st and 3d Friday of each month from 6:30 to 8:30 p.m.; The 2nd Saturday and Sunday of each month there are "How Did They Do That?" 30-minute workshops from 1 to 4 p.m. to show you how works of art were created.

Museum educators offer these tips to make any art museum more fun:

- Look closely at the art and encourage the kids to imagine the sights, sounds, and smells you would experience if you stepped inside.

- Strike a pose like a sculpture.

- Seek out artworks that portray kids.

- Create a theme. Search for faces, crowns, animals, or shapes.

A NYC KIDS SAYS:
"My favorite NYC museum is the Museum of the Moving Image because there's so many hands-on exhibits, and you can make your own stop motion clip."
—Marion, 12, NYC

- Bring along sketch pads and let the kids sketch what they see.

- Play "I Spy" in one gallery.

- Pick two different works of art and compare how they are similar and different.

- Leave when the kids—and you—have had enough, but keep the art conversation going. What was everyone's favorite?

Doughnut or Snail?

A lot of people thought the **Guggenheim Museum** (1071 Fifth Ave.; 212-355-4965; guggenheim.org) was a weird building when it was built. Some people thought it looked like a snail, others a doughnut. The building was designed as a spiral by famed architect Frank Lloyd Wright, with the art hung on the walls alongside a ramp. You may think some of these paintings are weird. Take the elevator to the top and look at the art as you head down the ramp.

The Cloisters (Fort Tryon Park at 193rd Street; 212-923-3700; metmuseum.org/visit/visit-the-cloisters) was put together from parts of buildings that date back to the 15th century! They were brought from Europe. Kids like to come to this branch of the Metropolitan Museum overlooking the Hudson River because they can play in the gardens and check out the brave knights and ferocious dragons on view. Don't miss the seven gigantic Unicorn Tapestries that were woven around 1500. How many plants can you count? There are images of more than 100.

The Museum of Modern Art
(11 W. 53rd St.; 212-708-9400; moma.org) is a great place to
see some masterpieces you've seen in school like Van Gogh's
The Starry Night, Picasso's *Les Demoiselles d'Avignon*, and Rodin's
great sculpture. Check out all the exhibits of appliances and
even sports cars as well as the Sculpture Garden.

Love history? Check out the **Museum of the City of
New York** (1220 Fifth Ave.; 212-534-1672; mcny.org), where
you'll especially like the exhibit of toys and dolls owned by
NYC kids and the New York Historical Society DiMenna
Children's History Museum, where you learn something about
NYC history through the eyes of kids who lived here at
different times in history [history.org. 70 Central Park West
at Richard Gilder Way (77th Street) New York, NY 10024;
212-873-3400].

DID YOU KNOW:

You can see children's art from around the world at the hands-
on **Children's Museum of the Arts** (between Greenwich and
Hudson Streets). Build creatures out of clay, learn how to animate
or record a song. Check out the Saturday Family Studios (103
Charlton St., New York, NY 10014; 212-274-0986; cmany.org).

4

Dinosaurs, Fighter Jets & Outer Space

THINK DINOSAURS. LOTS OF THEM!

The **American Museum of Natural History** (Central Park West at 79th Street; 212-769-5100; amnh.org) is home to one of the largest collections of vertebrate fossils—nearly one million in all!

This museum is the first one that many New York kids come to, and they return again and again. It's been here for more than 130 years, and like the Met, it's so huge you can't possibly see everything all at once. There are 25 buildings and 46 exhibition halls. Head to the fourth floor to see the dinosaurs. Say "hi" to the T. rex, apatosaurus, stegosaurus, and triceratops. Stop at some of the computers to find out more about these dinos. Make sure to see the dinosaur nest.

Kids also like to see the huge dioramas in the mammal halls on the first, second, and third floors that show you

DID YOU KNOW?

The **American Museum of Natural History** has a special website just for kids with activities and fun facts about science and the exhibits you can see at the museum. To find out about fossils, share discoveries with the scientists who made them and more, visit amnh.org/explore/ology.

the animals in their native habitats—they've got Alaskan brown bear, African elephants, water buffaloes from Asia, plus many others!

Don't miss the giant totem poles in the Hall of Northwest Coast Indians on the first floor, the museum's oldest hall. It opened more than a century ago in 1900!

You'll probably also want to see the giant 94-foot model of a blue whale. She weighs 21,000 pounds! You can find it on the first floor in the Milstein Hall of Ocean Life, and when you get there, you'll be staring at the biggest model of the biggest creature that ever lived on earth.

For ocean lovers, there are lots of other dioramas—of sea lions, dolphins, flying fish, and more. You can find hands-on activities about the living oceans in the Kids and Families section of the museum website, amnh.org.

If you like rocks, you'll love the Arthur Ross Hall of Meteorites, the Morgan Memorial Hall of Gems, and the Harry Frank Guggenheim Hall of Minerals. There are more than 100,000 rocks here. Make sure to stop and look at the Star of India. It's the world's biggest blue star sapphire. The topaz crystal from Brazil weighs 596 pounds. Check out the Cape York meteorite. It weighs 34 tons!

{ What's Cool? See the real exhibits behind the characters featured in the Night at the Museum movies at the American Museum of Natural History on the self-guided tour: amnh.org/plan-your-visit/self-guided-tours/night-at-the-museum-tour. There are other special tours, including the Dino Tour.

The Hayden Planetarium at the museum is really cool too. You'll feel like you're in a spaceship at the Space Theater! It's all part of the big seven-floor Rose Center for Earth and Space. Follow the Cosmic Pathway through 13 billion years; don't miss the chance to see the latest news from space and rock samples and models from around the world.

The museum's Hall of Biodiversity is the place to go to see why we should all care about the environment and how to protect all different kinds of life. This is where you can visit a diorama of a rain forest from Central Africa. It stretches for 90 feet, and you can step inside to see what happens to a rain forest when people don't take care of it. See all the leaves? There are more than 500,000 here, each made by hand! How about all the bugs?

If you're visiting around the holidays, you'll love the Origami Holiday Tree decorated with fanciful Japanese origami ornaments.

Make sure to allow plenty of time for the museum's Discovery Room on the first floor. Kids and their parents can get up close and personal with specimens, make their own exhibits, be part of a dinosaur "dig," solve puzzles, and even take apart and put together a big fossil.

WHAT DID YOU LEARN TODAY?

Check off what you saw at the American Museum of Natural History:

- ❑ T. rex
- ❑ A brown bear
- ❑ A Native American canoe
- ❑ A totem pole
- ❑ The Cape York meteorite, the largest meteorite in the world
- ❑ A rain forest
- ❑ A giant squid
- ❑ The blue whale, the world's largest animal
- ❑ A butterfly
- ❑ The planets of our solar system
- ❑ The Hayden Sphere
- ❑ A gem
- ❑ An elephant seal

Teddy Roosevelt

Got an annoying sibling?

Theodore Roosevelt's sisters hated his "finds"—assorted smelly animal carcasses, bird eggs, and more.

Theodore Roosevelt, of course, went on to be governor of New York and the 26th President of the United States. He was the nation's first conservationist-in-chief, responsible for protecting some 230 million acres of land, including 18 national monuments and five national parks.

But what a lot of people don't know is that he indirectly was involved in the founding of the American Museum of Natural History. The charter was signed in his boyhood home as his dad was one of the founders.

Roosevelt's relationships with the scientists here from the time he was a child helped shape his commitment to the environment. Check out the Theodore Roosevelt Memorial Hall when you visit the museum and see some of his collections from when he was a kid. Take a selfie with TR himself—well, his life-sized bronze sculpture.

A VISTING KID SAYS:
"The Intrepid Museum is my favorite museum in New York. Kids should get a small model of The Intrepid as a souvenir."
—Jake, 12, Weston, CT

Fighter Jets, Submarines, and Space Ships

Have you ever set foot on a giant aircraft carrier? Welcome to the **Intrepid Sea, Air & Space Museum** that is on the Aircraft Carrier Intrepid. More than 50,000 men served on board, starting during World War II.

Get a closeup look of the restored aircraft. It was hard to take off and land in the middle of the ocean! See where the sailors lived. Really tight quarters! Want to have a sleep over here?

This museum (Pier 86, W. 46th Street and 12th Avenue, New York, NY 10036; 212-245-0072; intrepidmuseum.org) is also the place to see the space shuttle Enterprise, the prototype NASA orbiter that paved the way for the space shuttle programs. Before you visit, you might want to download the Museum's free iPhone app Mission Intrepid: Explore Enterprise.

Walk underneath and see how big it is! Check out the Russian Soyuz TMA-6 space capsule. How are they different?

Climb aboard the *USS Growler*, a guided missile submarine, and see the once top-secret missile command center. Do you think you'd like living aboard a Sub?

Do you like to go really fast? The British Airways Concorde did in her day, crossing the Atlantic in less than three hours—supersonic speed!

Kid-Friendly Museum Events

There are some 150 museums in New York City. Here are the websites for some of the museums kids most like to visit in NYC. You can find links to others at nycgo.com.

American Folk Art Museum: Columbus Avenue at 66th Street; (212) 595-9533; folkartmuseum.org.

American Museum of Natural History: Central Park West at 79th Street; (212) 769-5100; amnh.org.

Brooklyn Children's Museum: 145 Brooklyn Ave., Brooklyn; (718) 735-4400; brooklynkids.org.

Brooklyn Museum: 200 Eastern Pkwy, Brooklyn; (718) 638-5000; brooklynmuseum.org.

Children's Museum of Manhattan: 212 W. 83rd St.; (212) 721-1223; cmom.org.

El Museo del Barrio about Latino culture: 1230 Fifth Ave.; (212) 831-7272; elmuseo.org.

Guggenheim Museum: 1071 Fifth Ave.; (212) 423-3500; guggenheim.org.

Intrepid Sea, Air & Space Museum: Pier 86, W. 46th Street and 12th Avenue; (212) 245-0072; intrepidmuseum.org.

Lower East Side Tenement Museum: 103 Orchard St.; (212) 982-8420; tenement.org.

Metropolitan Museum of Art: 1000 Fifth Ave.; (212) 535-7710; metmuseum.org.

Museum of Arts and Design: 2 Columbus Circle; (212) 299-7777; madmuseum.org.

Museum of Modern Art: 11 W. 53rd St.; (212) 708-9400; moma.org.

The Paley Center for Media: 25 W. 52nd St.; (212) 621-6600; paleycenter.org.

Museum of the City of New York: 1220 Fifth Ave.; (212) 534-1672; mcny.org.

Museum of the Moving Image in Queens: 36-01 35th Ave.; (718) 777-6888; movingimage.us.

National Museum of the American Indian: Alexander Hamilton U.S. Custom House, One Bowling Green; (212) 514-3700; nmai.si.edu.

New Museum: 235 Bowery; (212) 219-1222; newmuseum.org.

NYC's Jewish Museum: 1109 Fifth Ave. (at 92nd St.); (212) 423-3200; jewishmuseum.org.

TELL THE ADULTS:

- The American Museum of Natural History is one of New York's top tourist attractions.

- Be prepared for crowds! Come well fed and wearing comfortable shoes!

- Divide and conquer if the kids are interested in different exhibits. Amnh.org/learn-teach/families is a good resource for what the museum offers families.

- Go to The Discovery Room after you've seen some exhibits or the kids won't want to leave, as it offers the chance for hands-on activities.

- Take a Nature Walk with Museum scientists—including family bird walks and evening bat walks in central park.

- Astronomy Live programs at the Hayden Planetarium offer interactive tours of the universe and views of the changing night sky.

- Leave time at the end for the gift shops—including the ones tied to special exhibitions. The American Museum of Natural History has cool stuff for kids!

DID YOU KNOW?

The **American Museum of Natural History** has more than 33 million objects and specimens. The Metropolitan Museum of Art has more than 2 million objects in its collections. But not everything is on view at once. Both museums are on every family's top to-do list when they visit NYC. That's why there are more visitors from out of town here than New Yorkers. More people visit the two museums than live in most American cities.

5

PLAY BALL!

Anywhere you go in the city,

you're bound to see someone wearing a Yankees or Mets hat, a Knicks T-shirt, or maybe a Jets or Giants jersey.

New York City is home to millions of dedicated fans, whether the teams win or lose. There is also the chance to watch special sporting events such as college basketball tournaments, track and field championships, professional ice-skating, and even dog shows!

If you want to see a New York sporting event, **Madison Square Garden** (thegarden.com) is a great place to go. Located on Seventh Avenue between 31st and 32nd Streets, Madison Square Garden is the home of the New York Knicks basketball team (nba.com/knicks), **New York Rangers** hockey team (rangers.nhl.com), and the professional women's basketball team, **The New York Liberty** (wnba.com/liberty). The **Brooklyn Nets** basketball team (nba.com/nets) and the **New York Islanders** hockey team play at the Barclays Center in Brooklyn (620 Atlantic Ave., Brooklyn, NY 11217; 917-618-6100; barclayscenter.com.

A NYC KID SAYS:

"Make sure you go to a baseball game. They are always fun and full of energy. At Yankees games, during the 7th inning stretch, people come out and sing the YMCA song and it's fun to sing along."
—Sam, 13, NYC

Love tennis? Come in late August and early September for the **US Open Tennis Championship** (usopen.org) in Flushing Meadows.

Also, the MetLife Stadium in East Rutherford, New Jersey is where two famous New York football teams, the **New York Giants** (giants.com) and the **New York Jets** (newyorkjets.com), play.

New York City has two great baseball stadiums, which are home to two great ball clubs. There is Citi Field in Flushing, Queens, where the **New York Mets** play (newyork.mets.mlb.com) and Yankee Stadium, home to those Bronx Bombers, the **New York Yankees** (newyork.yankees.mlb.com).

If you go to a Mets or Yankees game, you have to try a stadium hot dog or ice cream. Who knows, maybe you'll catch a fly ball out in the stands! And, your face may even be put up on the big screen TV where everyone can see you! If you want this to happen, it's helpful to wear plenty of team gear and show some spirit!

A VISITING KID SAYS:
"I think the Yankees are my favorite team now. I really like the game and how big the stadium is!"
—George, 9, Australia

DID YOU KNOW?

The **New York Yankees** (newyork.yankees.mlb.com) and **New York Mets** (newyork.mets.mlb.com) are playing in stadiums that were built next door to where they previously played. So are the **Giants** (giants.com) and the **Jets** (newyorkjets.com) of the National Football League—they are sharing the new MetLife Stadium in New Jersey.

- Finding tickets to a New York sporting event is not as hard as some may think—although it does depend on what game you want to see. If you want to get them online, ticketmaster.com is a very simple way to find tickets, and there are many other websites that you can try as well. Or, you can try calling or going to the box office at the arena or stadium that is holding the event you want to see. You can often buy tickets from people selling them outside the stadium—but be careful. The prices you pay outside the stadium may be unreasonably high, and you could be getting a counterfeit ticket.

- If you can't get tickets to see the Yankees or the Mets, try a minor league team like the **Brooklyn Cyclones** (brooklyncyclones.com) on Coney Island.

- Ice-skating is expensive and crowded at **Rockefeller Center Ice Rink** outside Rockefeller Center, but it is really fun too (W. 49th Street and Fifth Avenue; rockefellercenter.com/tour-and-explore/the-ice-skating-rink/). There is also ice skating on the **Wollman Rink** in Central Park (830 5th Ave., New York ,NY 10065; 212-744-0882).

DID YOU KNOW?

The walkway leading into the arena at **Madison Square Garden** is now known as the "Walk of Fame" and recognizes performers, athletes, announcers, and coaches who have all demonstrated amazing things throughout their career, including Patrick Ewing (who played for the Knicks), and Wayne Gretzky and Mark Messier (who both played for the Rangers).

All city marathons are modeled on the **ING New York City Marathon.** Every year the NYC Marathon Team for Kids—runners from around the world—raises money on behalf of New York Road Runners youth services to help NYC kids be more active.

The Red Sox have never forgiven the Yankees for stealing Babe Ruth, so whenever the two teams play, it's considered a grudge match.

The **New York Botanical Garden** has a special Adventure Garden where kids can run around (2900 Southern Blvd., Bronx, NY; 718-817-8700; nybg.org).

Shop Till You Drop

New York is famous around the world for shopping. Here are some places NYC kids say you should go to find things you might not be able to get elsewhere:

Museum shops at the American Museum of Natural History

You'll find things from every exhibit; The Earth & Space, Cosmic, and Dino exhibits all have their own shops with special toys, science kits, and more. Central Park West & 79th Street, New York, NY 10024; (212) 769-5100; amnh.org

Exit 9 Gift Emporium

Exit 9, located in Brooklyn and Manhattan, sells build your own Empire State buildings alongside lots of funny souvenirs. 51 Avenue A, New York, NY 10009; (212) 228-0145; shopexit9.com.

By Brooklyn

One-of-a-kind made in Brooklyn gifts can be found here, even pickles. 261 Smith St. Brooklyn, NY 11231; (718) 643-0606; shop.bybrooklyn.com.

Memories of New York

Skip the crowds of Times Square and head to 23rd Street to find classic New York souvenirs—Empire State Building models, New York bags, postcards, or just about anything New

York themed. Check out the historic flatiron building on your way out! 206 5th Ave. New York, NY
10010; (212) 252-0030; memoriesofnewyork.com.

Brooklyn Flea

Vendors and shoppers come every Sunday to
this open air market with 100 vendors and 30 food
vendors too. 50 Kent Ave. Brooklyn, NY 11201;
(718) 885-1461; brooklynflea.com.

New York Transit Museum Gallery Annex & Store

There are exhibits and all MTA memorabilia for the
Brooklyn museum in Grand Central Terminal. Here's the place
for subway flip flops! Grand Central Terminal, 89 E. 42nd St.
New York, NY 10017; (212) 878-0106; grandcentralterminal.
com/store/new-york-transit-museum-gallery-annex-and-
store/2137026154 /2138781576.

Pylones

Where else can a toy princess be a cheese grater and
a hopping ladybug be a stapler? Every home item at Pylones
is disguised as a small cute animal, and there are toys too!
Grand Central Terminal, 87 E. 42nd St. New York, NY 10017;
(212) 867-0969.

Souvenir Smarts

A lot of kids like to get sports gear from NYC teams when they visit. Whatever you decide to buy:

- Shop smart! Talk to your parents about how much you can spend. Some families save loose change in a big jar to use for vacation souvenirs. It can really add up!

- Do you want to use your money for one big souvenir or several smaller ones?

- Resist impulse buys and think about choosing something you can only get in NYC.

- Start a collection! Buy stickers for your water bottle. Collect pins, patches, or keychains to put on your backpack.

What collection could you start?

Chelsea Piers—Come and Play!

If you're in New York and you're looking for a great place to take part in some sports, instead of just watching them, **Chelsea Piers Sports and Entertainment Complex** (chelseapiers.com) is the perfect place to head! Located between 17th and 23rd Streets along the Hudson River, Chelsea Piers contains a golf club, a sports center, a sky rink (ice rink), a field house, a roller rink, and a bowling alley. If you head on over to Chelsea Piers, you can take part in about any sport you can imagine, such as baseball, basketball, bowling, dancing, golf, gymnastics, ice hockey, ice-skating, in-line skating, rock climbing, roller hockey, skateboarding and BMX, and soccer. It's definitely a great place to meet other kids just like you and have lots of fun!

6
Grab the Smartphone
& Camera

Where can you go in the middle

of New York City and see five states? The Empire State Building, of course.

But maybe you'd rather ascend to the top of the tallest building in the Western Hemisphere—The One World Observatory downtown at One World Trade Center, 285 Fulton St. New York, NY 10007; (844) 6966-1776; oneworld observatory.com. Hear the stories of those who built this amazing building; step into the Sky Portal—a circular disc that promises to offer an unforgettable view. At City Pulse, there will be HD video monitors where you can get close-up views of the landmarks and neighborhoods below. You can even get something to eat! Ready to ride one of the fastest elevators in the world?

On a clear day you can see New Jersey, Connecticut, Pennsylvania, Massachusetts, as well as New York, from the Observatory on the 86th floor.

Of course New Yorkers still love the Empire State Building. It's one of the most recognizable of New York City's buildings. Everyone looks forward to seeing the colored lights on the Empire State Building from far away too—green for St. Patrick's Day; red, white, and blue for Independence Day; red and green for the holiday season; among others.

Be prepared to wait in line! Many people make the **Empire State Building** (350 Fifth Ave. between 33rd and

34th Streets; esbny.com) one of their must-see stops in New York. More than 100 million people have visited the top of the building. Some people even get married here.

You'll probably see parents and kids from lots of different countries at both places. When you enter One World Observatory's Global Welcome Center, there are greetings in many languages and a special map highlighting visitor's home towns.

In case you're wondering, the Empire State Building does get hit by lightning, about 100 times a year. It was designed to serve as a lightning rod for the surrounding area. When lightning strikes the tip of the Empire State Building, it travels directly—and harmlessly—down a metal conduit into the ground.

DID YOU KNOW?

The **Empire State Building** was built in just one year, winning the race (with the Chrysler Building) to be the world's tallest building at the time. The building is 1,453 feet, 8⁹⁄₁₆ inches tall.

One World Trade Center is 1,776 feet tall. It takes less than 60 seconds to get to the **One World Trade Center Observatory** on the 100th floor. Many believe that this building symbolizes NYC's strength and pride.

Need some exercise? There's a race up the 1,575 steps from the lobby to the 86th floor of the Empire State Building. Some runners have done it in just 10 minutes.

Wherever you check out the view, it's guaranteed to be an experience you'll want to remember. Ready for a selfie?

Another way to see all of New York's buildings is to sail around them—on a **Circle Line Tour** (Pier 83, W. 42nd Street; 212-563-3200; circleline42.com). Some tours around Manhattan Island take three hours and will give you plenty of opportunities to take pictures of the Statue of Liberty, the skyline, and the Brooklyn Bridge. There's a much shorter high-speed trip running from May to October kids like on *The Beast* where you race by all the skyscrapers (nytours.us). You've got to be 40" tall to ride. Ready for some more cool buildings? Stop in at the **Chrysler Building** (405 Lexington Ave.). The old-fashioned, art deco lobby is worth a stop because there aren't many like it. When Walter Chrysler built his skyscraper in 1930, he wanted the company's headquarters to make people think about his cars. The spire on top looks like a car radiator grille. There are decorations throughout the building that look like old-fashioned hood ornaments, wheels, and cars. Don't miss all the weird gargoyles on the building. There are even transportation scenes painted on the ceiling. How many can you find?

Stop in at **Grand Central Terminal** (42nd Street at Park Ave.; grandcentralterminal.com) while you're nearby. It's been a landmark since 1913. Half a million commuters use this terminal every day. It's a "terminal," not a "station," because every train begins or ends its journey here. See the clock at the central information area? It's got four faces. A lot of kids like to stop in Grand Central to get a snack (head downstairs to the big food court where you'll find food from around the world) and then look at the blue ceiling upstairs. It's a

DID YOU KNOW?

The Radio City Rockettes have been kicking up their heels in their world-famous chorus lines at **Radio City Music Hall** for more than 70 years (1260 Avenue of the Americas; radiocity. com). Since they started, more than 3,000 women have been Rockettes. The women all look like they're the same height, but it's an illusion. The tallest women are at the center with the shortest at either end. Besides performing in the Radio City Christmas spectacular, the Rockettes perform at the tree lighting ceremony at Rockefeller Center, during Macy's Thanksgiving Day Parade, and even the presidential inauguration.

painting of more than 2,500 stars. How many constellations can you find? Tip: little lights pinpoint them.

Quick! Think of a place in New York City where you can see your favorite music star, hear a gigantic dinosaur roar, or catch the latest news.

Stumped? Head directly to **Times Square.** At 42nd Street and Broadway, this is one of the easiest places in New York to reach by public transport since so many bus and subway lines stop here.

New York City kids like to come here because there's so much to do and see in just a few blocks. When your parents were kids, this part of town was so run down that families didn't like to walk around here much. The city has worked hard to clean up and rebuild Times Square in the last 15 years, and now it's usually the first place kids like to come when they visit New York! A lot of people say it's like

A VISITING KID SAYS:
"Make sure to go to Times Square and see all the lights. We went to see *The Lion King* and it was so much better than the movie."
—Jessie, 9, Boston, MA

a city theme park with cool restaurants, big stores (check out **M&M's World** on Broadway near 49th Street with every color of M&Ms you can imagine!), theaters, and even the world's largest TV screen. There are 12,500 hotel rooms here—one-fifth of all the rooms in the city—and more than 250 restaurants.

DID YOU KNOW?

Nearly 11 million visitors coming to New York each year are traveling with their families.

Times Square Scavenger Hunt: Can you find these things on your visit to Times Square?

❏ Hot pretzel

❏ Booth selling Broadway tickets

❏ A tourist with a camera

❏ The theater where *The Lion King* is playing

❏ The latest news flash

❏ An "I ♥ NY" T-shirt

Music Around the World

Anywhere you go in the city, you are bound to find it: New York is home to some of the greatest orchestras, operas, and ballet companies in the world. They welcome families with special performances just for them all through the year.

- Carnegie Hall (57th Street and Seventh Avenue; 212-247-7800; carnegiehall.org), has special family concerts as well as performances by young musicians

- The New York Philharmonic's Young People's Concerts nyphil.org/education/for-kids-and-teens/young-peoples-concerts)

- Chamber Music Society of Lincoln Center has a "Meet the Music!" series for kids and their families

- American Ballet Theater (abt.org) offers Saturday matinee pre-performance workshops for families

- The NYC Ballet offers one-hour presentations for families, featuring short works and excerpts from their repertory. (nycballet.com) At the holidays, many families make it a tradition to see the ballet's *Nutcracker* featuring many local children

- The Brooklyn Academy of Music (bam.org) has family workshops and concerts

- The Metropolitan Opera (metopera.org) has special kid-friendly performances of pieces like *Hansel and Gretel* and Mozart's *Magic Flute* at Lincoln Center

- Alvin Ailey American Dance Theater (alvinailey.org), has family weekend matinees

- The Brooklyn Academy of Music (bam.org) has lots of family workshops and concerts too

Festival Fever

Whenever you visit, there's a good chance there is some kind of festival, parade, or event that brings out the crowds:

January (or February)—**Chinese New Year** with parades and special feasts in Chinatown

March—**St. Patrick's Day Parade**, the biggest of all the city's parades

April—**Easter Day Parade** on Fifth Avenue with all kinds of crazy hats

May—**Martin Luther King Memorial Day Parade**

June—**Puerto Rican Day Parade**

July—**Independence Day Celebration**

September—**Feast Of St. Gennro** along Little Italy's Mulberry Street with all kinds of good eats

November—**The New York Marathon** and **Macy's Thanksgiving Day Parade**

December—The dropping of the giant ball in Times Square to celebrate the New Year at midnight, Dec. 31

Check out all the giant signs! Some are huge advertisements, but you can also read the latest news lit up on a moving stripe at One Times Square. Since the late 19th century, this has been the center of the country's theater world. And you can buy souvenirs from the street vendors or in one of the dozens of stores that line the streets.

Check out **Madame Tussaud's New York Wax Museum** (234 West 42nd St; 866-841-3505; nycwax.com), where you can "meet" Abraham Lincoln, Pharrell Williams,and Carmelo Anthony, among nearly 200 of their friends. Just one thing—they're all made of wax. It's not easy to pose for a wax portrait. Madame Tussaud's sculptors have to take lots of pictures and more than 250 measurements of each body. The sculptor models a clay portrait, and then the clay is molded in plaster. From that mold, the body is cast in fiberglass and the head from wax. Each pair of eyes is made individually— with hand-painted eyeballs

{ What's Cool? The New York Philharmonic's online Kidzone: nyphil.org/education/young-peoples-concerts/kidzone-online-learning

to match the real ones. Hair color is perfectly matched to a sample given by the celebrity and each strand is inserted one by one. The same goes with teeth. It takes five weeks just to make a head—six months to create the portrait. And every day, two teams inspect each figure to see if they need any "help" before the museum opens. They regularly get their hair washed and their makeup touched up! The celebrities often donate their own clothes and shoes, so the portraits will look more real. Got your camera? You can pose for a picture with your favorite star. They look so authentic your friends might be fooled. Tip: If you whisper in J-Lo's ear, she blushes!

While you're on 42nd Street, peek inside **Disney's New Amsterdam Theater** (214 W. 42nd St.; theater.disney.go.com/faq.html) a few steps west of Times Square. It's the city's oldest Broadway theater, having opened in 1903, before a lot of your grandparents were born! And it's been completely restored. This is where *The Lion King* opened on Broadway and is still playing to huge crowds.

You can visit all the little shops and street vendors selling "I ♥ NY" T-shirts, NYPD and NYFD hats, and replicas and key chains of the Statue of Liberty. What souvenir will you want to take home?

Lots of families like to see a play when they're in New City. You might get to go to one of the big Broadway theaters, or even see what is called an Off Broadway play. That means it's a smaller, less glitzy production, shown someplace other than the big Broadway theaters.

Tickets usually are cheaper too. Would you like to be an actor? Sometimes kids have parts in Broadway productions. They still have to go to school and do their homework, maybe in between their scenes. Sometimes they'll even move to New York City with their mom or dad temporarily to appear in a play. When they graduate from school, a lot of young people come to New York to audition for roles on Broadway. Many also work in restaurants as waiters or waitresses. Next time you're out at a restaurant, ask your server if he or she is an actor!

Sightseeing Smarts

New York is so big, and there's so much to do! You can't see it all. Here's how to have fun sightseeing:

Wear comfortable shoes.

Look at a map or program one into your phone so you know where you're going. (You can get a map at your hotel.)

Stash some snacks and a camera in your pocket.

Alternate sites you want to see like a museum or the Empire State Building with some people-watching, time in the park, or time out for a meal. That way you won't get so tired!

When you get really tired, take a break. You can go to a playground (there are more than 200 in the city!), get something to eat, or go back to the hotel and chill.

Alternate what you want to do and what your parents want you to see. That way everybody gets to lead the pack—some of the time.

Holiday Glitter

You've probably seen it on TV. There's been a big Christmas Tree in front of **Rockefeller Center** (rockefellercenter .com) since 1931! A special team goes all around the East Coast looking for the perfect tree. The Rockefeller Center Tree starts in someone's backyard where it's been growing for years and years. When asked, families donate the tree, which is then carefully brought into NYC with a police escort on a custom-made trailer. It takes at least 15 people and a 280-ton crane to handle the tree. More than 26,000 light-emitting diodes and five miles of wire decorate the tree. The same star has been used on top for more than 50 years. It's 5 feet wide! Of course the tree can be 100 feet tall. After the holidays, the tree is ground into mulch and used in the city's parks.

A VISITING KID SAYS:
"In the winter, it's really fun to go ice-skating at Rockefeller Center."
—Shelby, 9, NJ

Circus!

New York kids love the circus as much as kids everywhere. If you're visiting in the fall or winter, you might want to see the **Big Apple Circus,** the one-ring circus under a Big Top tent that's become a holiday tradition for New York families (Cunningham Park, 196-22 Union Turnpike, Queens, NY; 800-922-3772; bigapplecircus.com). There are acrobats, jugglers, dogs, clowns, flying trapeze artists, and more.

Ringling Brothers Barnum & Bailey Circus comes to New York City in the spring. Check ringling.com to see when the circus will be in town. There's also an area on the website for kids. A tip: Go early and you might be able to talk to the animals.

The United Nations

The United Nations Building (First Avenue between 42nd and 46th Streets; un.org) towers over the East River and is another must-see site. Your parents definitely will think so. The UN is the voluntary organization that countries around the world have joined to help keep peace, to develop friendlier relations among different countries, and to help poor people live better. Maybe you've collected pennies for UNICEF at Halloween time. That is a United Nations effort. Certainly you've heard about UN peacekeeping troops being sent to different countries around the world. Take a guided tour. You'll learn a lot about the work the delegates and staff do here as well as about the building. Have you ever seen so many people from so many different countries in one building?

DID YOU KNOW?

The pair of marble lions that stands outside the **New York Public Library** at Fifth Avenue and 42nd Street has been welcoming New Yorkers since the library opened in 1911 (nypl.org). First they were called Leo Astor and Leo Lenox, after New York Public Library founders John Jacob Astor and James Lenox. But during the 1930s, Mayor Fiorello La Guardia dubbed them Patience and Fortitude, for the qualities he thought New Yorkers needed to survive the Great Depression. And these names have stuck. Patience is on the south side of the steps and Fortitude on the north. If you visit at holiday time, they might have giant wreaths around their necks.

What's Cool? All of the lights in Times Square at night.

7

Lady Liberty &
Ellis Island

The Statue of Liberty

was a thank-you gift from France to the US that took more than 20 years to arrive.

And when she did come, she was packed in 214 crates, like a giant jigsaw puzzle that had to be put together. Good thing they sent directions along too.

But what a present the Statue of Liberty turned out to be! Originally planned as a gift of the people of France to the people of the US to commemorate their long friendship, she stands in New York Harbor as the most famous symbol of liberty and freedom in the world. She's also the biggest metal statue ever constructed.

A VISITING KID SAYS:
"I never really knew how big the Statue of Liberty is. And I like the boat ride to get there."
—Joey, 12, Chicago, IL

DID YOU KNOW?

The Statue of Liberty is green because it's made of copper and copper oxidizes when exposed to the air. It took 30 years for the statue to turn green!

When you're visiting the **Statue of Liberty** and **Ellis Island,** you're visiting a national park (nps.gov/stli). You can become a Junior Ranger at the Statue of Liberty or Ellis Island. Web Rangers is an online extension of the Junior Ranger program. (nos.gov/webrangers).

Immigrants cried when they saw her because they knew their long sea voyage was over. Today, a lot of people get choked up when they see Lady Liberty all lit up for the first time.

To get to the Statue of Liberty, you ride a ferry (201-604-2800; statuecruises.com) from Battery Park across New York Harbor to Liberty Island. It takes about 15 minutes, and then you can get back on the same ferry to visit Ellis Island.

The original idea was that the French people would build the statue and transport it to the US. The Americans were supposed to build the pedestal on which she would stand. The French raised the money they needed. But in the US, no one seemed to want to give any money to help. Finally, the *New York World,* a 19th-century newspaper, launched a big campaign to raise the needed funds. Even schoolkids contributed. People all around the country started to send money, and just

DID YOU KNOW?

A lot of the immigrants were kids traveling with their parents or older brothers and sisters. The very first person to be processed on Ellis Island was a 15-year-old girl, Annie Moore, who was traveling with her two brothers on January 2, 1892.

before the statue arrived in 1885, enough money had been raised to build the pedestal. She was unveiled the next year, in October 1886.

The sculptor Frédéric Auguste Bartholdi used his mom as the model for the Statue of Liberty's face. He spent more than 20 years on the project and put a lot of symbols into her. For example, the seven rays of her crown are supposed to represent the seven seas and the seven continents. The tablet she holds is engraved with the date of American independence, July IV, MDCCLXXVI (July 4, 1776), and her torch means she's lighting the way to freedom and liberty. At her feet are chains to symbolize her escaping the chains of tyranny.

On the second floor of the Statue Pedestal, you can see replicas of the statue's face and foot. They are big! And just think of the work it took to create this colossal statue.

She's made of copper sheets with an iron framework. It wasn't easy. The framework was designed and built by Gustave Eiffel, the great French engineer who later built the Eiffel Tower.

ELLIS ISLAND

Ellis Island is north of Liberty Island, about a 10- to 15-minute ferry ride on the Circle Line-Statue of Liberty Ferry from Battery Park. Maybe someone in your family arrived in the US here. Before 1892, individual states oversaw immigration, but as the numbers of immigrants increased, it got to be too big of a job.

The Great Hall, where the immigrants waited when they arrived on Ellis Island, is part of the museum. Look around. Do you think you would have been scared, not speaking the language, wearing clothes that looked different? Probably you would have been hungry and possibly sick after two weeks on a rocking boat.

A VISITING KID SAYS:
"The way New York looked from the boat going to see the Statue of Liberty was really cool!"
—Brandon, 9, Los Angeles, CA

Between 1892 and 1954, 12 million immigrants passed through Ellis Island. Each one had to pass a six-second medical exam in the Great Hall before they could enter the US to see if they had any of 60 different diseases like diphtheria, measles, or any other contagious illness or disability that would keep them from being able to earn a living. Ninety-eight percent passed.

It's important to remember that everyone who came to the US in those days didn't have to come through Ellis Island—not if they had more money. "Steerage," or third-class, passengers were the ones who landed here after upward of two weeks on crowded ships where they faced rough seas without much chance to get any fresh air.

DID YOU KNOW?

Over 100 million Americans trace their ancestry to those immigrants who passed through Ellis Island. Many immigrants still come to New York in search of a better life. People here in New York City come from nearly 200 different countries.

{ **What's Cool?** Visiting the Lower East Side Tenement Museum (108 Orchard St.; 212-982-8420; tenement.org), where you see what it was like for the immigrant families who lived and often worked in these tiny apartments. The museum is housed in an old tenement apartment building. Imagine going down four flights of steps to go to the bathroom outside!

When you visit Ellis Island, you can watch a movie about the immigrants who came here. Sometimes, professional actors bring to life the stories that immigrants have told over the years. Check when you arrive to see what time these plays start.

You might also get to see the reenactment of an immigrant hearing, just as it would have been conducted to determine whether the immigrant could stay in the US. Some of the exhibits might not be open, however.

Make sure to stop at the American Immigrant Wall of Honor, just outside the "peopling of America" exhibit. The

What's Cool? Going to the top of the Statue of Liberty crown or pedestal—the top of the pedestal is roughly half the height of the entire monument. There is no additional fee for the pedestal, but there is to go to the crown. You'll need advance reservations along with your ferry tickets (statuecruises.com/choose_tickets.aspx).

wall is inscribed with more than 600,000 names of those who came through Ellis Island. Families have paid to have their immigrant relative's names engraved.

You can really understand looking at all those different names from all those different countries and cultures why people call this country a melting pot. Your own family probably is one too. How many different countries do your relatives come from?

A lot of kids who come to NYC try food they haven't eaten at home. Check off what you've tried:

- ❏ a hot dog from a street vendor
- ❏ a hot salted pretzel or roasted nuts from a street vendor
- ❏ a slice of NYC pizza folded in half (that's the way New Yorkers eat it)
- ❏ a pastrami sandwich
- ❏ a fresh bagel with a shmear (of cream cheese)
- ❏ Chinatown noodles or rice with chopsticks

{ What's Cool? Trying a kind of food you've never tasted.

- If you come from a family of immigrants, you can look up a relative on the huge electronic database at the American Family Immigration History Center here. (libertyellisfoundation.org/family-history-center). There are ships' passenger records of more than 22 million people from 1892 to 1924, when immigration processing was at its peak at Ellis Island. These archives are now being expanded to include arrival in the Port of New York from 1925 through 1957.

- Before you come, gather as much information as you can, including first and last names, ethnicity and religion, approximate age on arrival, the ship, port of departure, and whether your relative was traveling with anyone else. If you find your relative's name, you can keep copies of the passenger records and chip images in a profile you can open by registering on Ellis Island, and you can purchase reproductions.

Grab a tape measure!

The height from the foot of the Statue of Liberty to the tip of the flame is 151 feet, 1 inch (from the ground, 305 feet, 1 inch). She weighs 225 tons (445,000 pounds). She's one big lady!

Her index finger: 8 feet

Her head: 17 feet, 3 inches

Nose: 4 feet

Right arm: 42 feet

Mouth: 3 feet wide (when she's not smiling)

A VISITING KID SAYS:
"Get a Statue of Liberty foam crown."
—John, 8, Greensboro, NC

DID YOU KNOW?

It's 354 steps from the entrance to the crown of the Statue of Liberty.

You get a terrific view of the Statue of Liberty on the free Staten Island Ferry across New York Harbor.

You've probably heard some of these words: "Give me your tired, your poor, your huddled masses yearning to breathe free." They're part of a very famous poem written in 1883 by Emma Lazarus. You can read the entire poem on a plaque in the statue museum.

Becoming a Citizen

The US is often called a melting pot or salad bowl because so many immigrants have come here from different countries and cultures looking for a better life. Many children whose parents are immigrants are citizens because they were born here. But just living here doesn't automatically make you a citizen. If you've come to the US from another country, to become a citizen you must:

- Be at least 18.

- Live in the US for five years or more.

- Be of good moral character and loyal to the US.

- Be able to read, write, and speak basic English to pass a test.

- Have enough basic knowledge of the US government and history to pass a test.

- Be willing to take an oath of allegiance to the US.

Once you've filed all the necessary documents and passed the tests, you appear before a judge and ask to become a citizen. You take a special oath. It's a very exciting day. Many immigrants live in the US their whole lives without becoming citizens.

Staying Safe on Vacation

Write down the name and phone number of the hotel where you're staying or put it in your phone. Make sure you have your parents' numbers too.

Practice "what if" situations with your parents. What should you do if you get lost in a museum? On a city street?

Decide when you arrive at a tourist destination on a central easy-to-locate spot.

If you get separated from your parents, only ask uniformed people for help—police officers, firefighters, store security guards or clerks, museum officials wearing official badges.

Pack Your Trunk!

When immigrants came in the last century, there was no e-mail, no TV, no Facebook, and most people didn't have telephones. The only way to find out more about life in America was by writing a letter to a relative already here. Sometimes, they exchanged photos so they'd know whom to look for when they arrived. Some teenagers came by themselves. If you were coming to America, you could only bring one small trunk with 30 things. You may be able to see some of what immigrants chose to bring with them in the Treasures from Home exhibit on the third floor of the museum on Ellis Island. What would you bring?

{ **What's Cool?** Walking around the Lower East Side and seeing what bargains you can find from the street vendors.

8

Yummy Foods, Giant Balloons & Bargains

Grab your chopsticks!

Everyone who comes to New York for the first time should have dinner in Chinatown. With the Chinese lanterns and telephone booths, and everyone speaking Chinese, it's like stepping into a Chinese city right in downtown New York. There are hundreds of restaurants to choose from.

You'll hear more Chinese spoken than English here in Lower Manhattan just south of Canal Street and a short walk from the Lower East Side. Even the street signs are in Chinese.

Browse in stores along Mott Street that sell Chinese toys, herbs, and all kinds of strange-looking foods. If you want to learn more about the history of Chinatown and the people

A NYC KID SAYS:
"I love eating in Chinatown. Try the pork or the crab, and if you pay attention, you can even learn how to use chopsticks!"
—Laurel, 11, Queens, NY

A NYC KID SAYS:

"There is this amazing candy shop called Dylan's Candy Bar." (Across the street from Bloomingdale's at Third Avenue and 60th Street. Dylandscandybar.com)–
"Every kid needs to try it!"
—Jason, 12, NYC

{ What's Cool? Counting how many different buses you've been on while in NYC. There are 4,373 buses, the world's largest fleet of buses.

who settled here, stop in at the **Museum of Chinese in America** (215 Centre St.; 212-619-4785; mocanyc.org).

Of course you're going to eat. The restaurants here are big—and tiny. Sometimes, the waiters don't speak English, but the menus often are printed in Chinese and English. Any kind of noodle dish is a good bet, New York kids say.

DID YOU KNOW?

The **New York Transit Museum** in Brooklyn (130 Livingston St) is the is the largest museum in the country devoted to urban public transportation history and offers special family programs. It has an annex in Grand Central Terminal. Learn more about NYC's subway stations by downloading a podcast tour at transitmuseumeducation.org/museumcast/.

A NYC KID SAYS:
"When you come to Little Italy, you should look around at the decorations in the streets. But what you have to do most is eat! I love it here."
—Nicholas, 9, NYC

They also like to come here on weekends for the Chinese brunch called dim sum. You pick all kinds of little dumplings from carts the waiters roll around the restaurant.

Little Italy is another old-fashioned neighborhood that's a favorite with kids and parents. It's just north of Canal Street and Chinatown. You'll find lots of little restaurants here too where you can have pizza, pasta, lasagna, and yummy Italian pastries and ice cream. Some families like to go to Chinatown for dinner and Little Italy for dessert. If you're visiting in September, all of Mulberry Street becomes a huge outdoor restaurant at the Festival of San Gennaro.

Of course you can get any kind of food you want in New York from an omelet in Greenwich Village to burgers in Midtown.

Girls like **American Girl Place** (609 Fifth Ave. at 49th Street; 877-247-5223; americangirl.com), where they come to buy dolls and doll clothes and books. It's fun to stay for tea or lunch at the cafe because their dolls get VIP treatment too and are served on special tiny china while sitting on doll-size seats. And everyone likes the loud, funky **Ruby Foo's** (1626 Broadway at 49th Street; 212-489-5600; rubyfoos.com).

Macy's Herald Square is still the world's biggest department store with 10 floors.

Kids think these stores are fun because they're like being in a giant treasure chest. Girls can try on makeup and perfume; boys can sample food. Everyone can check out the latest electronics at the **Sony Wonder Technology Lab** (550 Madison Ave.; 212-833-8100; sonywonder-techlab.com) or basketball gear at the **NBA Store** (590 Fifth Ave.; nba.com/nycstore/).

There's lots of special NYC gear too.

There are lots of other stores in NYC too—big ones and small ones. Even museums have great stores in New York. It's fun just to window-shop—and people-watch everywhere.

Don't forget your birthday money.

What's Cool? Eating a piping hot pretzel from a street vendor.

Macy's Thanksgiving Day Parade

Camels and elephants were part of the first Macy's Parade held on Thanksgiving Day 1924. Horses pulled the floats!

Today of course, the entire world watches the parade on TV, and millions of parents and kids line the route in New York City. There are bands—they compete from all over the country to get a spot—clowns, floats, singers, dancers including the Radio City Rockettes, and of course, the giant balloons.

A NYC KID SAYS:
"If you go to the Macy's Thanksgiving Parade, wear a lot of layers. It gets freezing!"
—Ronni, 9, NYC

The balloons have been a Macy's Parade tradition since 1927. In fact, to blow up the giant balloons Macy's uses more helium than anyone else in the country except the US government. A team of 10 artists works on designing and building the balloons all year long.

A lot of NYC kids like to go watch the balloons getting inflated the night before the Macy's Thanksgiving Day Parade. The balloons are rolled out and anchored with sandbags to keep them from flying away. (Hint: go to West 77th and 81st Streets between Columbus and Central Park West between 3 and 10 p.m.) The balloon lineup takes up two full city blocks.

TELL THE ADULTS:

Kids don't want to be limited to kids' menus, and you don't want them eating a steady diet of chicken fingers, fries, and mac and cheese on vacation. Vacation is a great time to try new foods, and it's not too hard to eat healthy along the way.

> **A NYC KID SAYS:**
> "Take the subway when you're in a hurry. They're the quickest and buses are slower."
> —Sarah, 9, NYC

1. Get the kids thinking about vacation as an adventure for their taste buds as much as a chance to explore new places. Let them pick the kind of food they want for dinner! You can search by the kind of food, price, or location on websites like yelp.com/c/nyc/restaurants.

2. Suggest that rather than ordering from the kids' menu, the kids order an appetizer or half portion from the regular menu.

3. Visit a farmer's market. There are more than 50 to choose from in New York, with over 230 family farms and fishermen participating. Especially in summer, you can find markets all around the city and buy what you need for a picnic in a park. Check out grownyc.org/greenmarket/ourmarkets.

A VISITING KID SAYS:
"I went shopping at Macys and it's huge and I loved it!"
—Victoria, 15, Sydney, Australia

4. Stash healthy snacks in your backpack.

Good Eats

FOR BBQ—Virgil's Real Barbeque near Times Square (152 W. 44th St., New York, NY 10036; virgilsbbq.com)

FOR PIZZA—John's Pizzeria (260 W. 44th St., New York, NY 10036; 212-391-7560; johnspizzerianyc.com)

FOR CHINESE—Chinatown (explorechinatown.com), west of the Bowery and south of Canal Street

FOR MAC AND CHEESE— Bubby's, which has plenty else on the menu (120 Hudson St., New York, NY 10013; 212-219-0666; bubbys.com)

FOR SINGING AND DANCING WAITERS—Ellen's Stardust Diner just near Times Square (1650 Broadway, New York, NY 10019; 212-956-5151; ellensstardustdiner.com)

FOR FUN SUSHI—East Japanese Restaurant, where you grab the rolls from the conveyor belt

(366 3rd Ave., New York, NY
10016; 212-889-2325; kara-
oke27.com/east_top.html)

FOR BURGERS—Bareburger,
   where you can get an elk
   burger, quinoa burger, and great grilled cheese
   and milkshakes. There are lots of locations
   (535 Laguardia Place, New York, NY 10012;
   212-477-8125; bareburger.com)

FOR SUNDAY BRUNCH—Sarabeth's, where you
   should try the french toast! There are a few locations, but this one, right across from Central Park,
   is great if you want to see the carriage horses
   or walk around the park (40 Central Park S, New
   York, NY 10019; 212-826-5959; sarabeth.com)

FOR FUN AND GAMES WHILE YOU EAT—Habana
   Outpost, a Mexican-Cuban Brooklyn cafe, has
   a kids corner every
   weekend from 11 a.m.
   to 3 p.m., with arts
   and crafts, music, and
   more (757 Fulton St.,

Brooklyn, NY 11217;
718-858-9500;
habanaoutpost.com)

FOR DELI—You'll find
delis everywhere
in NYC, but Katz's
Delicatessen is the city's oldest (205 E. Houston
St., New York, NY 10002; 212-254-2246; katzs-
delicatessen.com)

FOR ITALIAN—Little Italy (littleitalynyc.com),
where you have many restaurants to choose
from, and where you'll want to go to Ferrara for
dessert—Italian pastries and gelato (195 Grand
St., New York, NY 10013; 212-226-6150;
ferraranyc.com)

FOR THE ONLY NUTELLA BAR IN NYC—Eataly
NYC, where you might be able to watch an
Italian cooking demonstration, shop for a picnic,
and take your pick of seven restaurants (200
Fifth Ave., New York, NY 10010; 212-229-2560;
eataly.com)

FOR SWEETS:

Max Brenner Chocolate by the Bald Man—with fountains dripping different kinds of chocolate, as well as chocolate pizza, make your own s'mores, and much more (841 Broadway, New York, NY 10003; 646-467-8803; maxbrenner.com)

Ample Hills Creamery—Local kids think it's the best in the city. Check out the play area with books all about ice cream (305 Nevins St., Brooklyn, NY 11215; 347-725-4061; amplehills.com)

Economy Candy—Economy Candy has everything from old-fashioned candy shoelaces to Harry Potter's Chocolate Frogs to barrels of every gummy animal (108 Rivington St., New York, NY 10002; 212-254-1531; economycandy.com)

Dominique Ansel Bakery—Try the cronuts or the cookies shaped into a cup with milk inside! (189 Spring St., New York, NY 10012; 212-219-2773; dominiqueansel.com

Alice's Tea Cup—The most famous order here is the "Mad Hatter," which includes sandwiches, scones, cookies, and, of course, tea (156 East 64th St., New York, NY 10065; 212-486-9200; alicesteacup.com)

Dylan's Candy Bar—Come for chocolate souvenirs! (1011 Third Ave., New York, NY 10065; 646-735-0078, dylanscandybar.com)

M&Ms World—They'll have your favorite color and lots more! (1600 Broadway, New York, NY 10019; 212-295-3850; mmsworld.com)

Calling All Bargain Lovers

Every Sunday Orchard Street is closed to traffic from Delancey Street to E. Houston Street so merchants can put their merchandise out onto the street like in the old days. (Remember, Houston Street is pronounced, "HOW-ston street" by New Yorkers.)

More than 100 years ago, when immigrant families lived in the tall tenements in Lower Manhattan, peddlers hit the streets selling their wares out of potato sacks. They expanded to pushcarts and eventually storefronts selling everything from pots and pans to underwear to vegetables. The website for the Lower East Side area of stores and restaurants is lowereastsideny.com.

New Yorkers have always come to Orchard Street and the surrounding neighborhood looking for bargains. Today, they also come for cutting-edge fashion and great food like dill pickles, deli sandwiches, knishes, and more.

You'll still find great bargains on everything from leather jackets to purses to jewelry, perfume, and shoes. Don't be afraid to bargain: The storeowners expect it! Stop in at the **Lower East Side Tenement Museum** (108 Orchard St.; 212-982-8420; tenement.org).

9

Monkeys, Elephants, Polar Bears & Alice in Wonderland

Let's have some fun in the sun ...

or the snow. It doesn't matter. Central Park is the place New York kids go to play, and you can too.

There's plenty of room for sure. Central Park stretches for 50 city blocks between the Upper East and West Sides—843 acres smack in the middle of Manhattan.

It's been here for 150 years, since the city paid for a chunk of land that back then was virtually a dump. Today some New Yorkers pay just as much as the city did then for apartments just to overlook the park.

Maybe you'll want to take a horse-drawn carriage ride through the park. You'll see them lining up just outside the park on 59th Street, at the south end.

> **A NYC KID SAYS:**
> "You should definitely go to the merry-go-round and skate on Wollman Rink at night and go to the zoo—the polar bears are really cool."
> —Chris, 10, NYC

When you get to the park, stop in at **The Dairy** at the south end. In the 1870s, city children could get fresh milk here. Now the Victorian building is the Park Visitor Center and Gift Shop, where

A NYC KID SAYS:

"The best part about Central Park is all the cool shows they have there in the summer. And sometimes my parents take me to those operas on the big lawn. Those are cool because all my friends are there too."

—Kelly, 14, Manhattan

DID YOU KNOW?

There are 21 different playgrounds in **Central Park** and more than 200 across the city. The websitescentralparknyc.org and nycgovparks.org can steer you to all the city play lots.

Central Park is a great place to meet local kids.

you can pick up a map and find out what's happening in the park the day you're there.

Nearby, you'll find the **Wollman Rink** (wollmanskatingrink.com), where a lot of kids like to ice-skate in the winter. In the summer the rink is transformed into a little amusement park called **Victorian Gardens** (to get there enter Central Park from 59th Street and Sixth Avenue and walk north; 212-982-2229; victoriangardensnyc.com).

Central Park offers many concerts throughout the summer, and most of them are free. You can see shows ranging from some of your parents' favorite older artists to some of your favorite pop performers! So if you are going to be traveling to NYC in the summertime, you should check to see who is going to be playing in the park when you are there (centralpark.com/guide/activities/concerts.html). Maybe it will be someone you would like to see! Then check out the **Central Park Zoo** (at 64th Street and Fifth Avenue; centralparkzoo.com). You might get to see the polar bears tear open their Christmas presents.

A NYC KID SAYS:
"Every kid who visits NYC should not miss the Central Park Zoo. It's fun to see the animals!"
—Josh, 7, Brooklyn

DID YOU KNOW?

There are over 9,000 benches in Central Park. They would stretch 7 miles if placed end to end.

There are 24,000 trees and 250 acres of lawn in Central Park— plenty of places to run around!

You'll love the penguins, polar bears, sea lions, monkeys, and more. There's even a roaring waterfall and tropical birds.

There's a great playground near the Children's Zoo complete with a 45-foot spiral slide. Don't miss the George Delacorte Musical Clock. It's right near the Children's Zoo, and every hour a nursery rhyme plays while a bear with a tambourine, a hippo with a violin, a goat with panpipes, a kangaroo with horns, and a penguin with a drum glide around the base.

In the middle of the park at West 72nd Street, heading north, you'll pass Strawberry Fields. This is one of the park's most visited spots and was named to honor John Lennon, who lived nearby and could see this spot from his apartment building. It's an international peace garden with plants from every country in the world. Look for the mosaic in the pathway. It's inscribed with IMAGINE to remind people of the message of peace in Lennon's song.

A lot of kids also like to hang out in the **Sheep Meadow.** (Yes, there were sheep here in the park's first years.)

Cross a bridge yet? There are 36 bridges in the park—no two of them alike—and 58 miles of paths where you can walk, run, or ride horses and bikes.

The old-fashioned carousel is in the middle of the park at 64th Street. It's one of the biggest in the whole country!

Keep an eye out for **Alice in Wonderland.** You'll find her along with the Cheshire Cat, the Mad Hatter, and the Dormouse at the northern end of the Conservatory Water where kids and grown-ups like to sail model boats. Try sliding down her toadstool seat!

Kids also like the Hans Christian Andersen statue showing him reading "The Ugly Duckling." Kids like to climb onto the book—and the duck.

Say hi to **Balto the Dog** (at East 67th Street near the East Drive). Balto was the leader of the husky sled team that carried the serum across Alaska to save people from dying of diphtheria. Bet you didn't think you were going to learn a little history here in the park!

Of course, you'd probably prefer to run around, climb some rocks, or have a picnic under a tree. Where's the Frisbee?

While you're in the park, see if you can find these special things . . .

- ❏ Balto the sled dog
- ❏ Alice in Wonderland
- ❏ Mother Goose
- ❏ The carousel
- ❏ The Dairy
- ❏ A fancy fountain
- ❏ A police officer on a horse
- ❏ Strawberry Fields
- ❏ A bridge
- ❏ A polar bear

TELL THE ADULTS:

- The Central Park website, centralparknyc.org, can steer you in the right direction. And you can borrow or rent what you need.

- Rent in-line and roller skates at **Wollman Rink** on the East Side between 62nd and 63rd Streets, where you can also rent ice skates and skate in the winter.

- Rent bicycles, even two-seater tandems, at the **Loeb Boathouse** parking lot at East 74th Street, daily from March through October.

- Borrow a basketball to play at the **North Meadow Recreation Center**, mid park at 97th Street.

- Fish at the **Harlem Meer**, stocked with a wide variety of fish, at the northeast corner of the park.

- Rent a rowboat April through October at the **Loeb Boathouse** (East Side between 74th and 75th Streets) to take out on Central Park's 22-acre lake (thecentralparkboathouse.com).

- Play chess or checkers at the special tables inside the park at 65th Street just west of the Dairy, where you can borrow chess or checker pieces.

- Sail your own model sailboat at **Conservatory Water** (East Side between 72nd and 75th Streets) or call Central Park Sailboats at (917) 796-1382.

- You can also snooze under a tree, climb some rocks, chase your sister, or play Frisbee.

It Pays to Be Green

Got your reusable water bottle?

It will become a great souvenir when you slap stickers on it from all the places you've visited in New York. And you'll be helping the planet too instead of using disposable plastic water bottles.

You'll be helping the planet too when you take public transportation or walk in NYC. (The traffic is terrible anyway!)

The Wildlife Conservation Society, which oversees the Central Park Zoo and the Bronx Zoo, among others, sends scientists around the world to help endangered animals and inspire grownups and kids alike to value nature (wcs.org).

Here are some other simple things you can do to help the environment while you are in NYC:

- Turn off the lights and the air-conditioning when you leave your hotel room

- Recycle

- Reuse towels

- Take shorter showers

DID YOU KNOW?

More than 200 movies have included scenes in Central Park. Have you seen *Men in Black II, Stuart Little, You've Got Mail,* or *The Muppets Take Manhattan*? Can you name another one?

A VISITING KID SAYS:
"Don't miss the penguins at the Central Park Zoo. There's a good playground there too."
—Alex, 9, Chatham, NJ

{ What's Cool? The puppet shows at the Swedish Cottage Marionette Theatre at West 79th Street (212-988-9093).

10

The Freedom Tower, One World Observatory, a Memorial & Museum

September 11, 2001 . . .

that's such a long time ago for kids! Maybe you weren't born yet.

But your parents and grandparents certainly remember that awful day.

None of us can understand why someone would do something so terrible.

A NYC KID SAYS:
"It's hard for kids to understand but 9/11 affects all of us and it is important to know what happened."
—David, 16, NYC

This event changed all of our lives. We realize that every time we stand in a long line and take off our shoes to go through security at airports.

Now more than 10 years later, we can go to the 9/11 Memorial and remember and honor those who were killed.

DID YOU KNOW?

George Washington was inaugurated near the location of the 9/11 Memorial on Wall and National Streets, not in Washington DC. Look for the Federal Hall National Memorial that marks the spot.

{ What's Cool? Battery Park located on the southern tip of manhattan island facing new york harbor with great views of the Statue of Liberty and its own urban farm.

St. Paul's Chapel, part of the Parish of Trinity Wall Street in Lower Manhattan, became known as "The Little Chapel that Stood," as it is directly across from the World Trade

Center but wasn't damaged. It became a place for volunteers and first responders to rest. Today, tourists from around the world visit. There are memorial banners from around the world here.

DID YOU KNOW?

The **World Trade Center** once included seven buildings. When the World Trade Center was built in 1973, the 110-story Twin Towers became the tallest buildings in the world. Some 50,000 people worked here—more people than live in many suburban towns!

What's Cool? The high school museum ambassadors at the 9/11 Memorial Museum. You'll meet them at hands-on workshops for kids on Saturdays.

Now, we can go to the 9/11 Museum and Memorial and to remember and honor those who were killed and those who worked so tirelessly at the site.

Outside, there are two huge pools sitting in the original footprints of the Twin Towers— each is an acre—with huge waterfalls—the largest manmade water- falls in the country— surrounding them.

The museum is a serious place but a place

for kids too with drop-in activity stations tied to specific themes in the summer (check the museum's website at 911memorial.org for schedules)

You'll probably see kids from around the world here with their families. Everyone who visits New York wants to pay their respects.

Look at the massive artwork "Trying to Remember the Color of the Sky that September Morning." It's made up of 2,983 squares each painted a unique shade of blue in honor of those killed. See the Survivors' Stairs, one of two outdoor flights that were an escape route. You'll see the mangled Ladder Company 3 Truck, the huge destroyed elevator motor, and all kinds of artifacts—a fireman's hat, a shoe, ID cards. There are portraits and histories of those who died. Each person had a family and their own story.

When you get here, you're at the very bottom of Manhattan, the oldest part of New York City and the financial capital of the world. That's one of the reasons why the terrorists chose to attack the Twin Towers.

A VISITING KID SAYS:
"You can't come to the 9/11 Museum and not leave a different person."
—Chris, 15, Westport, CT

The **New York Stock Exchange** (nyse.com) and Wall Street are nearby. Growing numbers of people work here, and more people—including families—live nearby too, as new skyscrapers are being built—most recently **One World Observatory**, the tallest building in the Western Hemisphere.

You can visit the amazing observation deck seven days a week (One World Trade Center, 285 Fulton St., New York, NY 10017; 844-696-1776; oneworldobservatory.com). Tell your parents to get tickets in advance. All kids must be 6 or older. (Also see page 66.)

Spys Everywhere

George Washington took personal command of the Continental Army at New York in the summer of 1776. Early on, the British troops were successful and occupied the city, making it a political and military center as well as key to Washington's intelligence operation.

After hearing the Declaration of Independence on July 9, 1776, a crowd made its way down Broadway and tore down a large statue of King George III in the center of Bowling Green Park.

When You Visit

Be prepared for security screening, just like at the airport. You can't bring a large backpack or a bag bigger than 8" x 17" x 19", animals (except service animals), glass bottles, skateboards, or weapons.

A VISITING KID SAYS:
"I like thinking about how important it was that people tried to save other people that day. It makes me feel sad, but it's good to come here with your family."
—Jessie, 8, Orlando, FL

DID YOU KNOW?

In 1664, the city's tallest structure was a 2-story windmill!

The Survivor Tree

A Callery pear tree became known as the Survivor Tree after it lived through the September 11, 2001, terror attacks. It was discovered and freed from piles of rubble in the plaza of the World Trade Center and nursed back to health, despite a blackened trunk. It was planted at the memorial in December 2010 and hopefully will continue to grow among dozens of swamp white oak trees. When the memorial is complete, more than 400 trees will line the plaza—an urban forest!

What's Cool? Having a burger in Fraunces Tavern where George Washington told his troops goodbye after the American Revolution was won (54 Pearl St., New York, NY 10024; 212-425-1778; frauncestavernmuseum.org) Check out the museum, which re-creates rooms from that time!

TELL THE ADULTS:

Discussing 9/11 and other senseless terrorist attacks with kids isn't easy. But kids have a lot of questions, whether you visit the 9/11 Memorial and Museum or just hear about yet another terrorist attack on the news. Here is how the 9/11 Memorial experts suggest you start the conversation:

- LISTEN If the kids want to talk about either visiting the museum or their fears, offer them a safe place to share their questions. If they don't want to talk, don't force the discussion.

- DON'T AVOID DIFFICULT CONVERSATIONS It is the attacks themselves that are upsetting, not the conversations. Invite discussion with open-ended questions such as "What would you like to know about 9/11?" Reassure children about their own safety.

- ANSWER QUESTIONS WITH FACTS Children's recollections of 9/11 don't come from their memory, but rather school and the media, among other sources. It is important to answer children's questions with the basic facts.

What a Trip!

I came to New York with:

_____

_____

_____

The weather was:

_____

_____

_____

We went to:

_____

_____

_____

We ate:

_____

_____

_____

We bought:

_____

_____

_____

I saw these famous New York sights:

_____

_____

_____

My favorite thing about New York was:

_____

_____

_____

My best memory of New York was:

_____

_____

_____

My favorite souvenir is:

_____

_____

_____

_____

_____

_____

You had such a great time in New York!!! Draw some pictures or paste in some photos of your trip!!!

Index

```
S T S M U X O M D S D X Y R J E N
T I O A A H E M S N T L W K G T B
A M T N J L S G P Y A B Z A D H R
T E G H R V O W F T V L L W J E O
E S K A Q T H P I W R L S N Z B O
N S H T Z M O E E J I B D I O R K
I Q I T J H L S F V X Y N S N O L
S U E A Z T L R H H R L X R T N Y
L A V N T E K C Z V T G H L R X N
A R E I W K I G R O U N D Z E R O
N E L E X W Z E A F O H R N N X J
D M R E N E D I S M I D T O W N Q
H I H E M C H I N A T O W N E Q U
C T E V L O W E R E A S T S I D E
G R N T R C L W T X N V U H Q W E
G K T D T R I B E C A Q I M X O N
U N S P U O D W K B R N S F B R S
```

About the Author

Award-winning author Eileen Ogintz is a leading family travel expert whose syndicated "Taking the Kids" column is the most widely distributed in the country. She has also created TakingtheKids.com, which helps families to make the most of their vacations together. Ogintz is the author of seven family travel books and is often quoted as an expert on family travel in major publications such as *USA Today*, the *Wall Street Journal*, and the *New York Times*, as well as parenting and women's magazines. She has appeared on such television programs as *The Today Show*, *Good Morning America*, and *The Oprah Winfrey Show*, as well as dozens of local radio and television news programs. She has traveled around the world with her family, talking to other traveling families wherever she goes.